HISTORY OF THE DOBERMAN

Once upon a time, from 1834 to 1894 to be exact, there lived a man named Louis Dobermann. In the city of Apolda, state of Thuringia, country of Germany, he was a night watchman, dog catcher, and scavenger. And it is as unlikely that the man whose name became that of our breed set out deliberately to develop the breed that has become the Doberman Pinscher as if an old traditional men's tailoring firm should add a department for females' flimsies.

It is more likely that with the intense inbreeding of the times, which was mostly caused by the intolerably slow travel facilities, the breed just grew up.

William Sidney Schmidt has probably given more study to the origin and development of the Doberman Pinscher than anyone in modern times. It is his theory that Louis Dobermann just happened to be running the local dog pound and that people took some of "Dobermann's dogs"—and the name stuck. The people had a tendency to prefer good-sized, alert

Louis Dobermann, a German dog catcher in the late 1800s, is credited with the having this breed named for him.

watchdogs that thought went into the breeding that Dobermann did undoubtedly took those preferences into consideration.

Were our dog to be properly named, it is more appropriate that he be called the "Goeller Pinscher."

Otto Goeller was one of the very earliest breeders of the Doberman, and it is not at all improbable that he himself originated the breed as we now know it. Certainly he did much to stabilize the qualities of "Dobermann's dogs" that made them sought after. His systematic breeding and his intense interest in the breed make him, if not really the founder, the father of the Doberman Pinscher.

According to Schmidt, it was Goeller's opinion that the ancestry of the Doberman goes back to the old German Shepherd Dog, which should not be confused with the German Shepherds we see today, and to the large variety of the smooth-haired black and tan German Pinscher which is now extinct.

Other equally valid theories trace the Doberman to the Rottweiler, or butcher dog, and to the blood of hunting dogs, particularly the Weimaraner. It may also be claimed that the Doberman also owes allegiance to the French shepherd dog known as Beauceron or "red sock" because of its color and markings. It is also highly probable that breeds such as the Great Dane, the Setter, the Dachshund, and

Probably such breeds as the Great Dane, Setter, Dachshund and the Black-and-Tan Terrier were used in the creation of the Doberman.

Some authorities credit the Rottweiler as the ancestor of the Doberman Pinscher because of their colors.

the small, smooth-coated Black and Tan Terrier were used in the creation of the breed of the Doberman Pinscher and, during the early days, in refining qualities desired in the breed.

It was on August 27, 1899, that the National Doberman Pinscher Club was organized by Otto Goeller. It had its headquarters in Apolda. The first standard of the breed was written and the breed was given the name Doberman Pinscher. The breed was officially recognized as purebred—that is, the dogs were breeding true to type—by the Commission of Delegates in 1900. Recognition extended to the black and tan dogs only. A year later recognition was also given to the red and tan and to the blue and tan. The fawns or Isabellas were accepted even later. The American Kennel Club recognized the Doberman in 1908, and the first imports were exhibited in this country that year. It was a new breed and an exciting breed.

CHARACTER OF THE DOBERMAN PINSCHER

There have been a lot of things said about the Doberman Pinscher—some good and some bad; some in loving blindness and some in overstatement. The purpose here is to try to delineate the character of this truly great breed so that those readers who know and own Dobermans may understand them better and that those readers contemplating the ownership of a Doberman may have a better idea of what will happen to them and happen it will. What happens is simple. You bring the Doberman puppy into your home, he rides in your car, he sleeps on your hearth, he runs on your grounds, he is the playmate and guardian of your children. And you think how wonderful this all is! It really is, except that you've made an error in your summation of what happens. If you observe closely you'll realize that actually the Doberman loves to have you enjoy yourself in *his* home, he lets you drive *his* car, he sleeps on *his* hearth, he romps on *his* grounds, he plays with and protects *his* youngsters. All you really do is provide the wherewithal.

It is this sense of ownership that has, in our opinion, made the Doberman the preeminent protector and guardian, the loving and considerate lord of the manor that he is. And before the sun has set on the day he first comes home, you'll find you rather like the idea of being owned by your Doberman. It is highly probable that there is more loyalty to the breed by Doberman owners than by fanciers of any other breed— sometimes a fanatical loyalty, but always a loyalty.

Probably the one word that can best describe the character of the Doberman is "alert." And his alertness has no kin in fear or

PETS BY PAULETTE

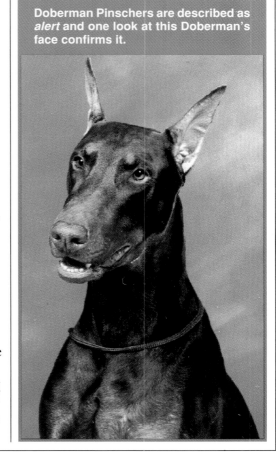

Doberman Pinschers are described as *alert* and one look at this Doberman's face confirms it.

shyness or braggadocio. His alertness is governed by a brain that has no superior among dogs for retention and the ability to reason. He is quick to learn and slow to forget. His consideration for the family that belongs to him is almost human in its quality.

But character goes beyond these attributes in the Doberman because it is so much a part of the whole dog. The Doberman is alert—in mind, in eye, in action. And he *looks* alert. The sight of a top-notch Doberman, in the show ring or at the driveway waiting for you to drive in, thrills the artist just as a great thoroughbred horse trotting by the clubhouse stand at the race track does. Here is balance; here is elegance; here is grace and eye-filling beauty; here is dignity in full measure. Yes, here is courage and strength and quickness.

Once it was considered sagacious to describe the Doberman as a "cocked pistol"— safe if you know what you're doing. This may have been true when the first Dobermans were imported from Germany to the United States, but that "hair-trigger" instability has been bred out of the modern American Doberman without decreasing his courage or his strength. It is probably more accurate to say

ISABELLE FRANCAIS/OWNED BY ELIZABETH KAMAV

The sight of an alert Doberman Pinscher on your front lawn is impressive and certainly inhibits trespassing.

The Doberman is alert in mind, eye and action...and he looks alert.

Dobermans are quiet unless provoked and aloof to strangers unless they violate his turf.

that if you expect to own a Doberman you'd better make sure you are smarter than he is.

As a matter of fact this is not a bad rule to apply in considering the purchase of any dog; there really aren't any bad dogs, just bad owners.

Most judges of dog shows can recall when the Doberman bench was the noisiest part of the arena. Today, as a result of work by the American breeders, the Doberman area is generally a quiet, peaceful bench. The Doberman is not inclined to bark without provocation; and his bark is always a warning. He is not a bully, but woe to the dog who starts a fight. To those he owns he is a clown with a delicious sense of humor, but to those outside he tends to be just a bit aloof and stand-offish. With outsiders in the home, chances are he'll sleep in the corner with one eye wide open. No harm shall come to his family, he seems to say. He means it, too.

Every one of us who has and loves Dobermans has heard the breed referred to as "vicious." Let's see why.

It is true that the Doberman is alert, brainy, and powerful. It is true that he made his great reputation primarily because of his outstanding abilities in police and guard work. It is true that he proved a valiant right hand to the US Marines during World War II.

It is true, to quote a feature on the breed that appeared in *Life* magazine, that the Doberman "is the color of anthracite and doom." It is true that he is used by many

Do you think anyone would enter this house uninvited? Dobermans are famous for their outstanding abilities in police and guard duties.

Dobermans are very friendly and playful with their owners. They are highly intelligent and easily trained. Training is a necessity.

of America's finest stores for after-hours patrol. It is true that more Dobermans are enrolled in sheriffs' departments throughout the nation than any other breed.

The Doberman Pinscher was created and developed to do these things for the benefit of mankind.

And most of the Dobermans you'll see performing their blood-bred duties could be called vicious by outsiders. That is because they were trained to perform these the enemy. He was taught strong loyalties to those who worked with him so that his obedience in the field was immediate.

Yes, a stranger approaching such a war dog would probably be justified in calling him "vicious."

By developing a tight, two-way loyalty and dark suspicions about everything else, it is possible to take a good specimen of almost any breed—including those with round, soft eyes and curly ears—

VINCE SERBIN

Many Dobermans are called *vicious* by their enemies because they are trained as guard dogs, war dogs and police dogs. In reality they are strongly protective and highly biddable.

duties. The first principle of such training is to develop strong *loyalties* and equally strong *suspicions*. For example, in order for a Doberman to extend the scope of his Marine handler on jungle patrol, it was essential that he be taught to be immediately suspicious of everything that smelled, looked, or sounded like and, make of him a dog which could also be called "vicious."

Dogs respond to love just as we do. Surround a dog with nothing but love, and you have a dog who wags his tail at anyone, who leads the intruder to the family silver. He has known love from everyone he has met and has no reason on earth to expect anything else from a stranger.

Conversely, if every person a dog ever sees treats him hatefully, the dog is bound to wind up as a dog who hates everyone. The trained-for-business Doberman must obey and must love in order to hate with discrimination. And that, then, is the secret of the Doberman doing his work for man. He discriminates between the good and the bad.

The two or three who work with

Doberman owners develop this reaction through extensive training mostly to see if they, the owners, can accomplish such results. It is also supposed that the same is true of owners of other breeds that were successfully used as war dogs. Such caressing of the human ego is sort of a shame. It has ruined many free dogs who would have been happier loving their families and letting their blood-bred

ROBERT PEARCY

Guard dog training requires strangers to provoke the Doberman until he attacks them. This man is a professional trainer.

him are always the same people. They are the ones who groom him, feed him, play with him. Every stranger is asked to deny the dog, to strike at him, scream at him, hit him. How logical it is then to understand why the Dobermans on night patrol willingly, anxiously, rush into mortal danger, on the command of a man they love, to rout out, hold, or, if commanded, attempt to kill the stranger they had learned to hate.

It is supposed that some

instincts and their blood-bred alertness and intelligence tell them how to discriminate between what is good and what is evil.

Therefore it is easy to see that the Doberman is alert, brainy, beautiful, and strong. He has great dignity. He is a loving companion and a faithful, devoted, and competent guardian of family and property. And if you are smart enough, you can make of him just about everything you could hope for in a dog.

Imagine two magnificent Dobermans walking up to greet you as you approach a friend's home. The gaping jaws are incidental as Dobermans cool off by exposing their tongues to the air. Dogs do not sweat the way humans do.

STANDARD FOR THE DOBERMAN PINSCHER

General Appearance—The appearance is that of a dog of medium size, with a body that is square. Compactly built, muscular and powerful, for great endurance and speed. Elegant in appearance, of proud carriage, reflecting great nobility and temperament. Energetic, watchful, determined, alert, fearless, loyal and obedient.

Size, Proportion, Substance— *Height* at the withers: *Dogs* 26 to 28 inches, ideal about 27 $^1/_2$ inches; *Bitches* 24 to 26 inches, ideal about 25 $^1/_2$ inches. The height, measured vertically from the ground to the highest point of the withers, equalling the length measured horizontally from the forechest to the rear projection of the upper thigh. Length of head, neck and legs in proportion to length and depth of body.

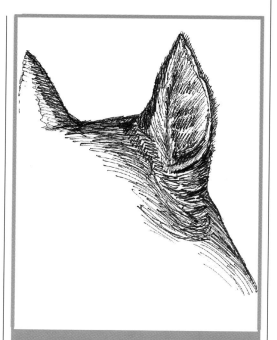

The Doberman's ears are normally cropped and carried erect, which is done by the surgical removal of a portion of the ear lobe. This practice is illegal in some countries, such as England and Australia. Drawing by John Quinn.

Head—Long and dry, resembling a blunt wedge in both frontal and profile views. When seen from the front, the head widens gradually toward the base of the ears in a practically unbroken line. *Eyes* almond shaped, moderately deep set, with vigorous, energetic expression. Iris, of uniform color, ranging from medium to darkest brown in black dogs; in reds, blues, and fawns the color of the iris blends with that of the markings, the darkest shade being preferable in every case. *Ears* normally cropped and carried erect. The upper attachment of the ear, when held erect, is on a level with the top of the skull. Top of *skull* flat, turning with slight stop to bridge of muzzle, with muzzle line extending parallel to top line of skull. Cheeks flat and muscular. *Nose* solid black on black dogs,

ISABELLE FRANCAIS

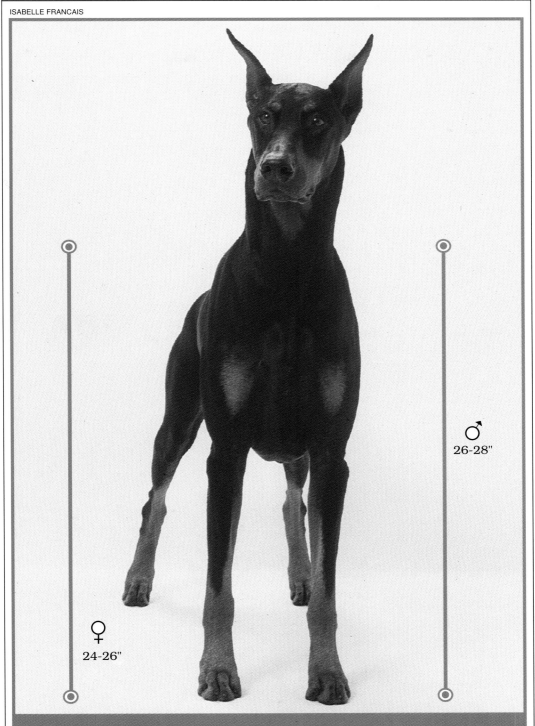

♂
26-28"

♀
24-26"

This dog won the Best of Breed at the 1994 Westminster Kennel Club Show. It is Ch. Royalmead's Prescot V Madori, owned by Ann E. Nelson, Ginanna Crouch, DVM and Joe Reid.

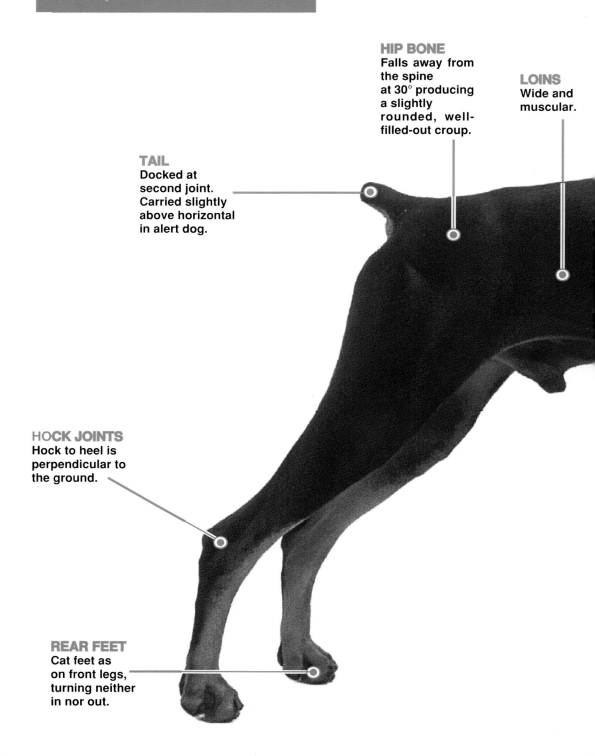

Ch. Royalmead's Prescott V Madori.
Best of Breed Winner 1994 Westminster
Kennel Club.
Owned by Nelson, Crouch and Reid.
Photo by Isabelle Francais.

HIP BONE
Falls away from
the spine
at 30° producing
a slightly
rounded, well-
filled-out croup.

LOINS
Wide and
muscular.

TAIL
Docked at
second joint.
Carried slightly
above horizontal
in alert dog.

HOCK JOINTS
Hock to heel is
perpendicular to
the ground.

REAR FEET
Cat feet as
on front legs,
turning neither
in nor out.

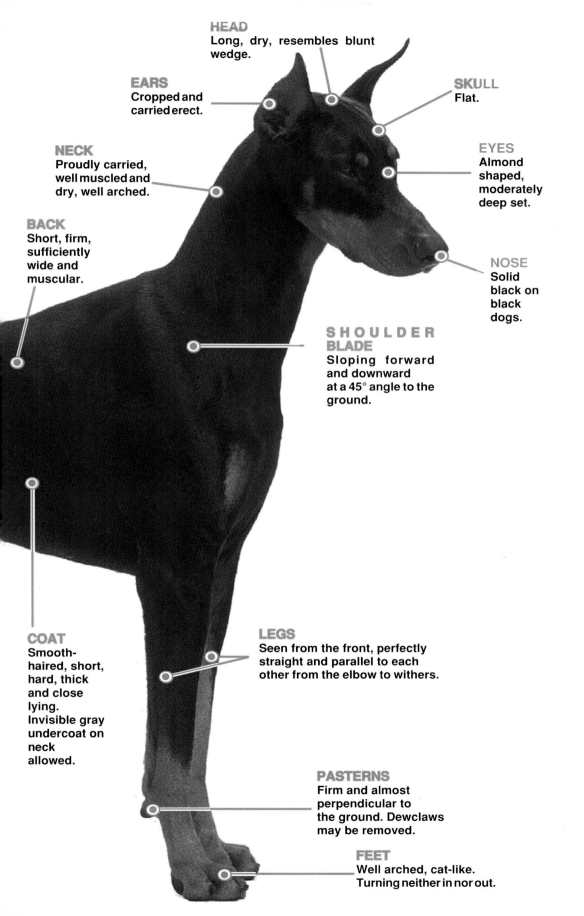

HEAD
Long, dry, resembles blunt wedge.

EARS
Cropped and carried erect.

SKULL
Flat.

NECK
Proudly carried, well muscled and dry, well arched.

EYES
Almond shaped, moderately deep set.

BACK
Short, firm, sufficiently wide and muscular.

NOSE
Solid black on black dogs.

SHOULDER BLADE
Sloping forward and downward at a 45° angle to the ground.

COAT
Smooth-haired, short, hard, thick and close lying. Invisible gray undercoat on neck allowed.

LEGS
Seen from the front, perfectly straight and parallel to each other from the elbow to withers.

PASTERNS
Firm and almost perpendicular to the ground. Dewclaws may be removed.

FEET
Well arched, cat-like. Turning neither in nor out.

dark brown on red ones, dark gray on blue ones, dark tan on fawns. Lips lying close to jaws. Jaws full and powerful, well filled under the eyes. **Teeth** strongly developed and white. Lower incisors upright and touching inside of upper incisors—a true scissors bite. *42 correctly placed teeth, 22* in the lower jaw, *20* in the upper. Distemper teeth shall not be penalized. *Disqualifying Faults*: Overshot more than $^3/_{16}$ of an inch. Undershot more than $^1/_8$ of an inch. Four or more missing teeth.

Neck, Topline, Body—*Neck* proudly carried, well muscled and dry. Well arched, with nape of neck widening gradually toward body. Length of neck proportioned to body and head. **Withers** pronounced and forming the highest point of the body. Back short, firm, of sufficient width, and muscular at the loins, extending in a straight line from withers to the slightly rounded croup. **Chest** broad with forechest well defined. **Ribs** well sprung from the spine, but flattened in lower end to permit elbow clearance. **Brisket** reaching deep to the elbow. **Belly** well tucked up, extending in a curved line from the brisket. **Loins** wide and muscled. **Hips** broad and in proportion to body, breadth of hips being approximately equal to breadth of body at rib cage and shoulders. **Tail** docked at approximately second joint, appears to be a continuation of the spine, and is carried only

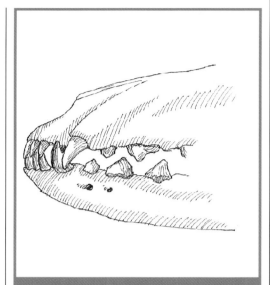

The Doberman Pinscher has a true scissors bite. The outer surfaces of the lower incisor teeth engage with the inner surfaces of the upper incisors when the mouth is shut. Drawing by John Quinn.

slightly above the horizontal when the dog is alert.

Forequarters—*Shoulder Blade* sloping forward and downward at a 45-degree angle to the ground meets the upper arm at an angle of 90 degrees. Length of shoulder blade and upper arm are equal. Height from elbow to withers approximately equals height from ground to elbow. **Legs** seen from front and side, perfectly straight and parallel to each other from elbow to pastern; muscled and sinewy, with heavy bone. In normal pose and when gaiting, the elbows lie close to the brisket. **Pasterns** firm and almost perpendicular to the ground. Dewclaws may be removed. **Feet** well arched, compact, and catlike, turning neither in nor out.

ISABELLE FRANCAIS

Allowable colors for Dobermans are as follows: black, red, blue and fawn (Isabella). Their markings must be rust and only in designated areas of the body.

Hindquarters—The angulation of the hindquarters balances that of the forequarters. **Hip Bone** falls away from spinal column at an angle of about 30 degrees, producing a slightly rounded, well filled-out croup. **Upper Shanks** at right angles to the hip bones, are long, wide, and well muscled on both sides of thigh, with clearly defined stifles. Upper and lower shanks are of equal length. While the dog is at rest, hock to heel is perpendicular to the ground. Viewed from the rear, the legs are straight, parallel to each other, and wide enough apart to fit in with a properly built body. Dewclaws, if any, are generally removed. **Cat feet** as on front legs, turning neither in nor out.

Coat—Smooth-haired, short, hard, thick and close lying. Invisible gray undercoat on neck permissible.

Color and Markings—*Allowed Colors*: Black, red, blue and fawn (Isabella). *Markings*: Rust, sharply defined, appearing above each eye and on muzzle, throat and forechest, on all legs and feet, and below tail. White patch on chest, not exceeding $1/2$ square inch, permissible. *Disqualifying Fault*: Dogs not of an allowed color.

Gait—Free, balanced, and vigorous, with good reach in the forequarters and good driving power in the hindquarters. When trotting, there is strong rear-

The tan spots on the cheeks of the Doberman Pinscher are called kiss marks. Drawing by John Quinn.

ISABELLA FRANCAIS

Luckily both dogs are restrained with leads. When Dobermans have an aggressive or belligerent attitude toward another dog, it is NOT considered a vicious trait.

action drive. Each rear leg moves in line with the foreleg on the same side. Rear and front legs are thrown neither in nor out. Back remains strong and firm. When moving at a fast trot, a properly built dog will single-track.

Temperament—Energetic, watchful, determined, alert, fearless, loyal and obedient. *The judge shall dismiss from the ring any shy or vicious Doberman. Shyness*: A dog shall be judged fundamentally shy if, refusing to stand for examination, it shrinks away from the judge; if it fears an approach from the rear; if it shies at sudden and unusual noises to a marked degree. *Viciousness*: A dog that attacks or attempts to attack either the judge or its handler, is definitely vicious. An aggressive or belligerent attitude toward other dogs shall not be deemed viciousness.

FAULTS
The foregoing description is that of the ideal Doberman Pinscher. Any deviation from the above described dog must be penalized to the extent of the deviation.

DISQUALIFICATIONS
Overshot more than $3/16$ of an inch. Undershot more than $1/8$ of an inch. Four or more missing teeth. Dogs not of an allowed color.

YOUR NEW DOBERMAN PUPPY

SELECTION

When you do pick out a Doberman Pinscher puppy as a pet, don't be hasty; the longer you study puppies, the better you will understand them. Make it your transcendent concern to select only one that radiates good health and spirit and is lively on his feet, whose eyes are bright, whose coat shines, and who comes forward eagerly to make and to cultivate your acquaintance. Don't fall for any shy little darling that wants to retreat to his bed or his box, or plays coy behind other puppies or people, or hides his head under your arm or jacket appealing to your protective instinct. *Pick the Doberman Pinscher puppy who forthrightly picks you! The feeling of attraction should be mutual!*

ROBERT PEARCY

Take your time in selecting a Doberman puppy. The longer you study the puppies in a litter, the wiser will be your choice. If a puppy selects you, buy it!

DOCUMENTS

Now, a little paper work is in order. When you purchase a purebred Doberman Pinscher puppy, you should receive a transfer of ownership, registration material, and other "papers" (a list of the immunization shots, if any, the puppy may have been given; a note on whether or not the puppy has been wormed; a diet and feeding schedule to which the puppy is accustomed) and you are welcomed as a fellow owner to a long, pleasant association with a most lovable pet, and more (news)paper work.

GENERAL PREPARATION

You have chosen to own a particular Doberman Pinscher puppy. You have chosen it very carefully over all other breeds and all other puppies. So before you ever get that Doberman Pinscher puppy home, you will have prepared for its arrival by reading everything you can get your hands on having to do with the management of Doberman Pinschers and puppies. True, you will run into many conflicting opinions, but at least you will not be starting

If the mother or father of a puppy is a champion, you can expect a better puppy, which also means a more expensive puppy. The pedigree usually has little to do with a Doberman's value *as a pet*.

"blind." Read, study, digest. Talk over your plans with your veterinarian, other "Doberman Pinscher people," and the seller of your Doberman Pinscher puppy.

When you get your Doberman Pinscher puppy, you will find that your reading and study are far from finished. You've just scratched the surface in your plan to provide the greatest possible comfort and health for your Doberman Pinscher; and, by the same token, you do want to assure yourself of the greatest possible enjoyment of this wonderful creature. You must be ready for this puppy mentally as well as in the physical requirements.

ISABELLE FRANCAIS

When you get home with a new Doberman puppy, put him on the floor, preferably in the kitchen where an accident is more easily cleaned up. If you put him in YOUR bed, you are asking for a problem!

TRANSPORTATION

If you take the puppy home by car, protect him from drafts, particularly in cold weather. Wrapped in a towel and carried in the arms or lap of a passenger, the Doberman Pinscher puppy will usually make the trip without mishap. If the pup starts to drool and to squirm, stop the car for a few minutes. Have newspapers handy in case of car-sickness. A covered carton lined with newspapers provides protection for puppy and car, if you are driving alone. Avoid excitement and unnecessary handling of the puppy on arrival. A Doberman Pinscher puppy is a very small "package" to be making a complete change of surroundings and company, and he needs frequent rest and refreshment to renew his vitality.

THE FIRST DAY AND NIGHT

When your Doberman Pinscher puppy arrives in your home, put him down on the floor and don't pick him up again, except when it is absolutely necessary. He is a dog, a real dog, and must not be lugged around like a rag doll. Handle him as little as possible, and permit no one to pick him up and baby him. To repeat, *put your Doberman Pinscher puppy on the floor or the ground and let him stay there except when it may be necessary to do otherwise.*

Quite possibly your Doberman Pinscher puppy will be afraid for a while in his new surroundings, without his mother and littermates. Comfort him and reassure him, but don't console him. Don't give him the "oh-you-poor-itsy-bitsy-puppy" treatment. Be calm, friendly, and reassuring.

Mother and child, both excellently trained and magnificent in behavior, are worth much more than an untrained, nonconforming puppy. You will have the Doberman for a long time, maybe up to 15 or more years, so take time to select the best puppy you can afford.

Encourage him to walk around and sniff over his new home. If it's dark, put on the lights. Let him roam for a few minutes while you and everyone else concerned sit quietly or go about your routine business. Let the puppy come back to you.

Playmates may cause an immediate problem if the new Doberman Pinscher puppy is to be greeted by children or other particularly to a Christmas puppy, when there is more excitement than usual and more chance for a puppy to swallow something upsetting. It is a better plan to welcome the puppy several days before or after the holiday week. Like a baby, your Doberman Pinscher puppy needs much rest and should not be over-handled. Once a child realizes that a puppy has

These puppies may be for sale. They are of two different colors but came from the same mother. One is active and one is passive. Which best suits your lifestyle?

PETS BY PAULETTE/OWNED BY CAROL KEPLER

pets. If not, you can skip this subject. The natural affinity between puppies and children calls for some supervision until a live-and-let-live relationship is established. This applies "feelings" similar to his own, and can readily be hurt or injured, the opportunities for play and responsibilities provide exercise and training for both.

For his first night with you, he

should be put where he is to sleep every night—say in the kitchen, since its floor can usually be easily cleaned. Let him explore the kitchen to his heart's content; close doors to confine him there. Prepare his food and feed him lightly the first night. Give him a pan with some water in it—not a lot, since most puppies will try to drink the whole pan dry. Give him

HOUSEBREAKING HELPS

Now, sooner or later—probably sooner—your new Doberman Pinscher puppy is going to "puddle" on the floor. First take a newspaper and lay it on the puddle until the urine is soaked up onto the paper. *Save this paper.* Now take a cloth with soap and water, wipe up the floor and dry it well. Then take the wet

Puppies kept outside have usually not been housebroken. They will *piddle* on the floor once they are kept inside your home unless you train them. It usually takes less than a week to housebreak a Doberman since they are both intelligent and naturally clean.

PETS BY PAULETTE/OWNED BY CAROL KEPLER

an old coat or shirt to lie on. Since a coat or shirt will be strong in human scent, he will pick it out to lie on, thus furthering his feeling of security in the room where he has just been fed.

paper and place it on a fairly large square of newspapers in a convenient corner. When cleaning up, always keep a piece of wet paper on top of the others. Every time he wants to "squat," he will seek out this spot and use the papers. (This routine is rarely necessary for more than three days.) Now leave your Doberman Pinscher puppy for the night. Quite probably he will cry and howl a bit; some are more stubborn than others on this matter. But let him stay alone for the night. This may seem harsh treatment, but it is the best procedure in the long run. Just let him cry; he will weary of it sooner or later.

ISABELLE FRANCAIS/OWNED BY BLUM*

An untrained Doberman is a nightmare; a trained Doberman is a dream. Wouldn't you be proud to own a Doberman that looks like this one? It's all a matter of training!

It requires training to educate your Doberman as to the proper place to defecate, but it can be done.

ISABELLE FRANCAIS

PETS BY PAULETTE/OWNED BY CAROL KEPLER

OK, you've gotten your Doberman puppy home. Do you know what to do with it? For sure, you should let it spend the first night alone...even if it howls and cries. The loneliness wears off in a night or two and you will have started the puppy's training without even realizing it.

When you buy a Doberman puppy, the color is unimportant providing it agrees with the standard (if you intend to show the dog or use it for breeding). Color has nothing to do with personality. Sit in front of a group of Doberman puppies. If one comes to you, take it home. If none comes to you, your decision must be based upon personality. If you want an active dog, buy an active puppy.

ISABELLE FRANCAIS/OWNED BY LINDA HOFF

It is advisable to walk your Doberman on a lead whenever he leaves the house or your fenced-in yard. Well-trained Dobermans have been known to bolt after a cat or another dog before they hear your command to STOP!

EXERCISE AND ENVIRONMENT

Let's first discuss environments that are suited to the well-being of our Doberman Pinscher. It would be nice, we suppose, if we could say that here is a dog which thrives in the arctic and thrives on the Equator, who conditions himself to any locale where man can live.

Sure, the Doberman can get along just about every, place a human can, but it would be better if we'd discuss his strong points as well as his weak ones insofar as his happy climate is concerned.

Generally you can assume that the Doberman will do well in any temperate climate. He does not do well in extreme heat or in extreme cold. His coat is just not heavy enough to give him proper insulation against the real extremes in climate. He does better in a fairly dry climate than in one with constantly high humidity.

We wrote earlier of the Doberman's successes as a war dog. He worked through the terribly hot and humid climate of

At the 1995 World Dog Show in Brussels, Dobermans were shown on a loose, choke-collar lead parading in front of the judges. This was proof to the judges that the dogs had been trained and exercised and that they suffered no apparent maladies.

When exercising your dog, even when showing him at a competition, always have water available for him. Your hand will make a nice drinking fountain if there is nothing else available.

the Solomon Islands with the Marines. He did a wonderful job as almost any combat Marine will tell you. But he sometimes suffered miserably doing it. The reason? His short coat just wasn't barrier enough for the biting flies, mosquitoes, and other obnoxious insects that thrive in places like Guadalcanal.

Your Doberman will love a good long romp in the snow. But he is not sufficiently insulated to spend

or Guyana, our advice to you is don't buy a dog of any breed.

So, now with one swift stroke, we have eliminated about $1/10{,}000$ ths of the earth's population. Because there just aren't that many Dobermans to go around we'll discuss environment in a more personalized manner.

City dog or country dog? You can't lay down a generality here that will make sense to everybody. This is because the circumstances

PETS BY PAULETTE

This Doberman puppy has had its ears cropped and is recuperating. This is NOT the time for strenuous exercising. Let him rest with his toys.

hour after hour in zero-degree weather. None of the short-coated breeds are.

So, if you live in Nome or in Rabaul, don't buy a Doberman. If you live in the first named, you'll be happier with an Alaskan Malamute, an Eskimo, or Samoyed, among others. And if you live in Rabaul or Port Darwin

of city living for some people may be an ideal environment for their Doberman while the "country living" of others might not suit him at all.

For example, a city family with adequate quarters for a Doberman, the leisure to take him for a couple of good walks every day, and the ability to take him some place at least once or twice a week where he can run free and romp gaily for an hour or so would be an ideal family for a Doberman to own. We know many families such as the one generally described above whose Dobermans are as happy and healthy as one could imagine.

warmth of their family.

A Doberman would probably call the perfect life one in which he enjoyed the privileges of running free on a fenced acre or so and the right to come into the house to relax with his family when he chose.

Owning any dog is a

ISABELLE FRANCAIS

The ideal home for a Doberman is one in which he has a fenced-in yard in which to exercise, and a bed inside the house so he can stay close to the family he loves.

Why do we not go whole hog for the country life as being the perfect environment for the Doberman? Primarily because we believe that fundamentally the Doberman is a home dog. It has been our experience that although Dobermans will run and romp for hours they also like to find a quiet place where they can nap in the

responsibility. The happy, healthy dog is the one whose family recognizes and responds to this responsibility. We certainly do not intend to make this chapter a deterrent to those considering the purchase of a Doberman. But facts are better faced before the purchase than dismayingly faced afterward.

Exercising is as necessary for you as it is for the dog. Dobermans can easily run faster, farther and longer (timewise) than any human being.

Older people should walk at least 30 minutes five times a week. What better situation than exercising their Doberman at the same time...the dog also protects as it accompanies.

GROOMING

Your Doberman should be groomed every day. But let's be realistic and set a minimum of three days a week for this job. And it needn't be a chore if you'll do it properly. Here is the equipment you should have bought when you first brought him home: 1) one rubber massage brush, 2) one grooming brush (the glove kind with soft wire bristles is excellent), 3) one pair of nail clippers (the kind that works on a guillotine principle is best), 4) a towel that is too far gone for further use, and 5) one pair of sharp scissors.

Now Monday, Wednesday, and Saturday, say, you will groom your Doberman. Mondays and Wednesdays will take five minutes, Saturdays, a maximum of 15 minutes. Keep him standing and go over him thoroughly with the rubber massaging brush. Chances are he'll love it. Then brush him strenuously with the glove brush. Rub him down with the towel; double-check to make certain his eyes, ears, toes, and the pads of his feet are clean and you're finished for Mondays and Wednesdays.

On Saturdays you do exactly the same except that, every Saturday you clip his toenails.

Believe us, this is important. Our dogs today just don't wear their nails down enough to keep them tidy. We doubt if they ever did; we feel it was rather an unbalanced diet that kept them broken off so that a good dog's feet were kept in shape. Today we must keep his nails short. Take them down as close to the quick as you can and do this every week.

Once a month you'll want to trim him so that he looks like everything a Doberman should. Whiskers, ears, flank, and tail can be done in another five minutes. It does nothing for his health, but how can you estimate what it does for his self-esteem?

One further tip here on grooming. You've undoubtedly noticed many, many dogs with balding spots on their elbows and hocks. This is not unusual with the medium-sized and larger

ISABELLE FRANCAIS/OWNED BY NANCY BASLEY

Is there a more beautiful sight than a well-conditioned Doberman in a show pose? Training and conditioning are necessary to develop a dog like this.

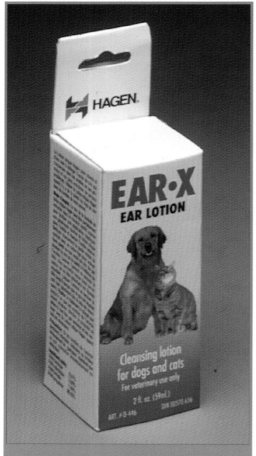

Specially designed ear-care products for your Doberman are sold through most pet shops. Photograph courtesy of Hagen.

and capable of holding a coat. Show dog or not, we have made it a part of our regular grooming routine.

Bathing? It is up to the reader. We don't. That is, most of the time we don't. With regular grooming as we've discussed you may well never have to bathe your Doberman. Here is one of the cleanest animals God has created. But if he should come in a little on the smelly side, use the prepared dry shampoos made especially for dogs. You rub it in and

VINCE SERBIN

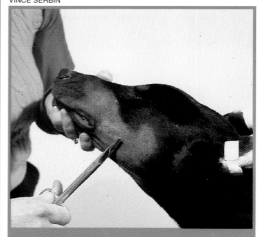

Unsightly facial hairs should be removed with special scissors available from your pet shop.

breeds. They are caused by the sheer weight of the dog being supported by elbows and hocks when he is lying down. Unless they become heavily calloused or infected because of a turned hair which becomes ingrown, such bald spots are no cause for alarm, but they are unsightly. They do not help his appearance on the street or in the show ring.

The regular application and rubbing in of one of the lanolin products will keep the skin soft

brush it out and he'll smell as if he'd been resting on pine needles all of his life. If you're on the seashore and he takes a daily swim in the ocean, he'll need a hosing off with fresh water. But, fundamentally, keeping your Doberman clean is a matter of judgment. We urge you to use good judgment in this regard.

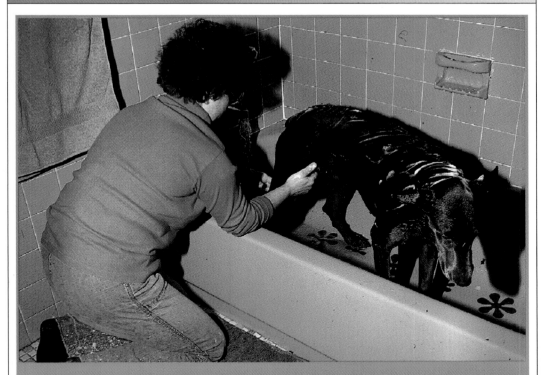

Bathing your Doberman can be a hassle, or it can be easy. It depends upon how you train him. Having him stand in the bathtub while you first soap him and then rinse him makes the job simple and fast. The Doberman is too strong to force into a bathtub or into standing for soaping and rinsing.

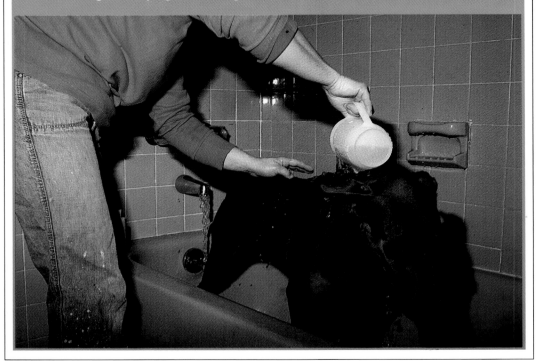

EAR CROPPING

The ears of a Doberman Pinscher are normally cropped and carried erect in all countries where ear cropping is permissible. In those countries where this practice is against the law, as in Great Britain, Australia, etc., the ears remain uncropped and carried in their natural position. It is agreed that there is considerable difference in the expression of a Dobe with cropped ears and one whose ears are natural; and the feeling is that for show purposes, the erectly carried, cropped ears are generally more becoming. Of course a dog imported from a country where ear cropping is legal can be shown in those countries where it is not, provided that the dog is accompanied by a certificate from the veterinarian stating that the operation was performed in a legal manner.

It is a matter of standard recommendation that a Doberman's ears be cropped. In the UK, Australia and other places, it is illegal to have a Doberman's ears cropped. Do you think cut ears look better than drop ears?

Not all Dobermans have their ears cropped.

The cropped ear is carried erect with the upper attachment, when ears are at attention, on a level with the top of the skull. It is important that the ear cropping be done with skill and expertise, as there is no more certain way of ruining a Dobe's appearance (and, if a show prospect, his possible future career) than with an inept, unsuccessful ear cropping job. Ears incorrectly cropped can be left too long (which at least may be correctable with a second and perhaps third operation), too short, not truly matching, and not well carried. As this is a cosmetic operation, you want the dog to come through it with graceful, well-balanced, well-carried ears that will enhance his beauty and his expression. So no matter

A Doberman puppy after having its ears cropped, being isolated in a crate for its own protection.

ISABELLE FRANCAIS

If the surgery is desired, Doberman puppies have their ears cropped at around seven or eight weeks. You can see that mother's ears have an attractive, smart look.

what, never be tempted to take any chances with the possibility of someone "messing up" on the job.

Ideally, of course, you should find yourself a puppy with ears already cropped and standing. If this cannot be done, the next best thing would be to put a deposit on a puppy and leave it with the breeder until its ears have been cropped and are standing as they should. This also may be impossible, in which case, before arranging the ear cropping yourself, make every effort to locate someone whose work in this regard you have seen or can see, one who comes recommended by either the puppy's breeder or someone else experienced in raising show-type Dobe puppies.

Please bear in mind that as the

ISABELLE FRANCAIS

A magnificent Doberman head featuring cropped ears. Would it be so elegant if the ears were not cropped? This is the magnificent Best of Breed winner of the 1994 Westminster Show.

ears heal from being cropped, the aftercare shares almost equally in importance with the actual cropping. During this period the ears must be kept taped and protected in order that they heal quickly and completely and be carried correctly. Unless you are familiar with the procedure, assistance from experienced Doberman fanciers will prove invaluable.

You will find considerable discussion and advice on the subject of ear cropping and aftercare in another book on this breed, *The World of Doberman Pinschers*, also published by T.F.H. Publications, Inc.. *The World of Doberman Pinschers* is a very large, very complete and comprehensive study of the breed, in which any and all questions you may have pertaining to Dobermans are fully answered.

THE WORLD OF DOBERMAN PINSCHERS is an excellent and comprehensive book on the breed. This book is available at your local pet shop.

This lovely Doberman is from England and does not have its ears cropped. There is active debate about whether ear cropping is a necessity. It is simply a matter of taste. Dobermans with cropped ears look more attentive and that may be a plus for their use as guard dogs.

TRAINING

You owe proper training to your Doberman Pinscher. The privilege of being trained is his birthright; and whether your Doberman Pinscher is going to be a handsome, well-mannered housedog and companion, a show dog, or whatever possible use he may be put to, the basic training is always the same—all must start with basic obedience, or what might be called "manner training."

Your Doberman Pinscher must come instantly when called and obey the "Sit" or "Down" command just as fast; he must walk quietly at "Heel," whether on or off lead. He must be mannerly and polite wherever he goes; he must be polite to strangers on the street and in stores. He must be mannerly in the presence of other dogs. He must not bark at children on roller skates, motorcycles, or other domestic animals. And he must be restrained from chasing cats. It is not a dog's inalienable right to chase cats, and he must be reprimanded for it.

PROFESSIONAL TRAINING

How do you go about this training? Well, it's a very simple

KAREN TAYLOR

Doberman Pinschers are highly intelligent animals and can be trained to do anything any other dog can do. The photo shows a Doberman on a obstacle course clearing an agility bar jump.

ISABELLE FRANCAIS

A Doberman must be trained to sit, stay and stop upon command before he is allowed off the lead.

procedure, pretty well standardized by now. First, if you can afford the extra expense, you may send your Doberman Pinscher to a professional trainer, where in 30 to 60 days he will learn how to be a "good dog." If you enlist the services of a good professional trainer, follow his advice of when to come to see the dog. No, he won't forget you, but too-frequent visits at the wrong time may slow down his training progress. And using a "pro" trainer means that you will have to go for some training, too, after the trainer feels your Doberman Pinscher is ready to go home. You will have to learn how your Doberman Pinscher works, just

Training your dog to *shake hands* is a job for your kids. Kids like their dogs to shake hands, but there is much more important training to be learned.

what to expect of him and how to use what the dog has learned after he is home.

OBEDIENCE TRAINING CLASS

Another way to train your Doberman Pinscher (many experienced Doberman Pinscher people think this is the best) is to join an obedience training class right in your own community. There is such a group in nearly every community nowadays. Here you will be working with a group of people who are also just starting out. You will actually be training your own dog, since all work is done under the direction of a head trainer who will make suggestions to you and also tell

ISABELLE FRANCAIS

It is not too difficult for your Doberman to be trained to carry your purse, bring your slippers or get the daily newspaper. Enroll him (and yourself) in an obedience training class. It is time well spent.

VINCE SERBIN

Training the Doberman puppy is not always easy. It takes time and patience to teach any dog tricks, but walking on a lead is NOT a trick, it is a necessity!

you when and how to correct your Doberman Pinscher's errors. Then, too, working with such a group, your Doberman Pinscher will learn to get along with other dogs. And, what is more important, he will learn to do exactly what he is told to do, no matter how much confusion there is around him or how great the temptation is to go his own way.

Write to your national kennel club for the location of a training club or class in your locality. Sign up. Go to it regularly—every session! Go early and leave late! Both you and your Doberman Pinscher will benefit tremendously.

VINCE SERBIN

JUDITH STROM

Below: If you came to a closed gate and you saw a Doberman's snout sticking out like this, would you enter? You'd be foolish if you did. That's why Dobermans have such high value as guard dogs.

Above: For special training, a Doberman is often the breed of choice. Police often use Dobermans and have special schools in which to train the dogs and the officers who work with them.

Leashes, like these, are retractable with the push of a button and can be locked to a fixed length. These leads are necessary for the training of your Doberman and are available at your local pet shop. Photograph courtesy of TRAKT.

TRAIN HIM BY THE BOOK

The third way of training your Doberman Pinscher is by the book. Yes, you can do it this way and do a good job of it too. If you can read and if you're smarter than the dog, you'll do a good job. But in using the book method, select a book, buy it, study it carefully; then study it some more, until the procedures are almost second nature to you. Then start your training. But stay with the book and its advice and exercises. Don't start in and then make up a few rules of your own. If you don't follow the book, you'll get into jams you can't get out of by yourself. If after a few hours of short training sessions your Doberman Pinscher is still not working as he should, get back to the book for a study session,

ROBERT PEARCY

Dobermans have to be trained to hate and attack. This training involves the dog being provoked by a stranger with hits, hollers and howls.

because it's your fault, not the dog's! The procedures of dog training have been so well systemized that it must be your fault, since literally thousands of fine Doberman Pinschers have been trained by the book.

After your Doberman Pinscher is "letter perfect" under all conditions, then, if you wish, go on to advanced training and trick work.

Your Doberman Pinscher will love his obedience training, and you'll burst with pride at the finished product! Your Doberman Pinscher will enjoy life even more, and you'll enjoy your Doberman Pinscher more. And remember— you *owe good training to your Doberman Pinscher.*

ISABELLE FRANCAIS/OWNED BY KAREN REAMS

Training your Doberman to sit and wait is important. He can be guarding your car, your chair, your space, or simply be waiting for you outside the shopping center.

Dobermans have to be trained to attain and maintain a show pose.

SHOWING YOUR DOBERMAN PINSCHER

A show Doberman Pinscher is a comparatively rare thing. He is one out of several litters of puppies. He happens to be born with a degree of physical perfection that closely approximates the standard by which the breed is judged in the show ring. Such a dog should, on maturity, be able to win or approach his championship in good, fast company at the larger shows. Upon finishing his championship, he is apt to be as highly desirable as a breeding animal. As a proven stud, he will automatically command a high price for service.

ISABELLE FRANCAIS

The number, cleanliness and appearance of your Doberman's teeth are important factors in the show ring. The Doberman must have 42 teeth, 20 in the upper jaw and 22 in the lower jaw.

Showing Doberman Pinschers is a lot of fun—yes, but it is a highly competitive sport. While all the experts were once beginners, the odds are against a novice. You will be showing against experienced handlers, often people who have devoted a lifetime to breeding, picking the right ones, and then showing those dogs through to their championships. Moreover, the most perfect Doberman Pinscher ever born has faults, and in your hands the faults will be far more evident than with the experienced handler who knows how to minimize his Doberman Pinscher's faults. These are but a few points on the sad side of the picture.

The experienced handler, as I say, was not born knowing the ropes. He learned—*and so can you!* You can if you will put in the same time, study and keen observation that he did. But it will take time!

KEY TO SUCCESS

First, search for a truly fine show prospect. Take the puppy home, raise him by the book, and as carefully as you know how, give him every chance to mature into the Doberman Pinscher you hoped for. My advice is to keep your dog out of big shows, even Puppy Classes, until he is mature. Maturity in the male is roughly two years; with the female, 14 months or so. When your Doberman Pinscher is approaching maturity, start out at match shows, and, with this experience for both of you, then go gunning for the big wins at the big shows.

Next step, read the standard by which the Doberman Pinscher is judged. Study it until you know it by heart. Having done this, and you now know by heart.

In your evaluations, don't start looking for faults. Look for the virtues—the best qualities. How does a given Doberman Pinscher shape up against the standard? Having looked for and noted the virtues, then note the faults and see what prevents a given Doberman Pinscher from standing correctly or moving well. Weigh these faults against the virtues,

JOHN ASHBEY

The most prestigious of American dog shows is the Westminster Kennel Club show. The thrill, prestige and financial rewards for winners is unmatched in the dog world.

while your puppy is at home (where he should be) growing into a normal, healthy Doberman Pinscher, go to every dog show you can possibly reach. Sit at the ringside and watch Doberman Pinscher judging. Keep your ears and eyes open. Do your own judging, holding each of those dogs against the standard, which since, ideally, every feature of the dog should contribute to the harmonious whole dog.

"RINGSIDE JUDGING"

It's a good practice to make notes on each Doberman Pinscher, always holding the dog against the standard. In "ringside judging," forget your personal preference for this or that feature. What does the standard say about it? Watch carefully as the judge places the dogs in a given class. It is difficult from the ringside always to see why number one was placed over the second dog. Try to follow the judge's reasoning. Later try to talk with the judge after he is finished. Ask him questions as to why he placed certain Doberman Pinschers and not others. Listen while the judge explains his placings, and, I'll say right here, any judge worthy of his license should be able to give reasons.

When you're not at the ringside, talk with the fanciers and breeders where the Doberman Pinschers are benched. Don't be afraid to ask opinions or say that you don't know. You have a lot of listening to do, and it will help you a great deal and speed up your personal progress if you are a good listener.

THE NATIONAL CLUB
You will find it worthwhile to join the American Doberman Pinscher Club and to subscribe to its magazine. From the national club, you will learn the location of an approved regional club near you. Now, when your young Doberman Pinscher is eight to ten months old, find out the dates of American Kennel Club match shows in your section of the country. These differ from regular shows only in that no championship points are given. These shows are especially designed to launch young dogs (and young handlers) on a show career.

ENTER MATCH SHOWS
With the ring deportment you have watched at big shows firmly in mind and practice, enter your Doberman Pinscher in as many match shows as you can. When in the ring, you have two jobs. One is to see to it that your Doberman Pinscher is always being seen to its best advantage. The other job is to keep your eye on the judge to see what he may want you to do next. Watch only the judge and your Doberman Pinscher. Be quick and be alert; do exactly as the judge directs. Don't speak to him except to answer his questions. If he does something you don't like, don't say so. And don't irritate the judge (and everybody else) by constantly talking and fussing with your dog.

In moving about the ring, remember to keep clear of dogs beside you or in front of you. It is my advice to you *not* to show your Doberman Pinscher in a regular point show until he is at least close to maturity and after both you and your dog have had time to perfect ring manners and poise in the match shows.

ISABELLE FRANCAIS/OWNED BY NANCY BASLEY

Your Doberman must be able to attain his stance upon command if you expect great successes at a dog show.

ISABELLE FRANCAIS

The winner with his ribbons and trophy. But the real winnings come with stud fees! This dog took Best in Show!

YOUR DOBERMAN'S HEALTH

We know our pets, their moods and habits, and therefore we can recognize when our Doberman Pinscher is experiencing an off-day. Signs of sickness can be very obvious or very subtle. As any mother can attest, diagnosing and treating an ailment require common sense, knowing when to seek home remedies and when to visit your doctor...or veterinarian, as the case may be.

Your veterinarian, we know, is your Doberman Pinscher's best friend, next to you. It will pay to be choosy about your veterinarian. Talk to dog-owning friends whom you respect. Visit more than one vet before you make a lifelong choice. Trust your instincts. Find a knowledgeable, compassionate vet who knows Doberman Pinschers and likes them.

Grooming for good health makes good sense. The Doberman's close-lying, hard and thick coat benefits from regular brushing to keep looking glossy and clean. Brushing stimulates the natural oils in the coat and also removes dead haircoat. Dobermans shed seasonally, which means their undercoat (usually invisible) is pushed out by the incoming new coat. A medium-strength bristle brush and a hound glove are all that is required to groom this beautiful breed of dog.

Anal sacs, sometimes called anal glands, are located in the musculature of the anal ring, one on either side. Each empties into the rectum via a small duct. Occasionally their secretion becomes thickened and accumulates so you can readily feel these structures from the outside. If your Doberman Pinscher is scooting across the floor dragging his rear quarters, or licking his rear, his anal sacs may need to be expressed. Placing pressure in and up towards the anus, while holding the tail, is the general routine. Anal sac secretions are characteristically foul-smelling, and you could get squirted if not careful. Veterinarians can take care of this during regular visits and demonstrate the cleanest method.

Many Doberman Pinschers are predisposed to certain congenital and inherited abnormalities, such as hip dysplasia, a blatantly common problem in purebred dogs with few exceptions. Unfortunately, the Doberman Pinscher suffers from a high percentage rate of hip dysplasia despite the efforts of many conscientious breeders. This is due to the breed's considerable popularity and the careless breeding that surrounds the procreation of popular breeds. New owners must insist on screening certificates from such hip registries as OFA or PennHIP. Since HD is hereditary, it's necessary to know that the parents and grandparents of your puppy had hips rated good or better. Dysplastic dogs suffer from badly constructed hip joints which become arthritic and very painful, thereby hindering the dog's ability to be a working dog, a good-moving show dog, or even a happy, active pet.

Wobbler syndrome (cervical vertebral instability) can affect dogs four to ten years of age. It can vary greatly in severity from moderate limping to complete paralysis.

Von Willebrand's disease, a bleeding disorder, and hemophilia A are conditions that affect many dog breeds and do not exclude the Doberman Pinscher. Some kidney problems are reported along with an inherited metabolic liver defect.

For Doberman Pinscher breeders, the most pressing health concern is cardiomyopathy, a heart condition that affects an increasing number of Dobermans. Cardiomyopathy is recognized in two forms: dilated and hypertrophic, the former of which more commonly affects the Doberman. The condition is characterized by a thin, over-stretched heart muscle that no longer is able to pump effectively. Such dogs suffer from heart failure. Some veterinarians suggest that the dilated condition is associated with nutrition. Amino acid supplementation may be beneficial. The condition, when diagnosed, can be treated through medicine and drugs which work to strengthen the heart.

Hypothyroidism (malfunction of the thyroid gland) can be linked to many symptoms in Dobermans,

such as obesity, lethargy, and reproductive disorders. Supplementation of the thyroid decreases problems, though such dogs should likely not be bred.

Despite these potential problems, a well-bred Doberman is a healthy, long-lived companion animal. Proper care and education can only help owners promote the health and longevity of their dogs. Most breeders advise against feeding the Doberman Pinscher one large

PETS BY PAULETTE/OWNED BY STEVE NILES

A healthy Doberman *looks* like a healthy dog. This youngster exudes health, alertness and discipline.

meal per day because of the dangers of bloat (gastric torsion): the twisting of the stomach causes gas to build up and the organ expands like a balloon. Avoiding strenuous exercise and large amounts of water can preclude the occurrence of bloat, as can feeding two smaller meals instead of one larger one. A good commercial dog food is recommended for the dog's balanced diet. Buy it in a petshop as it's ususlly fresher and of higher quality.

For the continued health of your dog, owners must attend to vaccinations regularly. Your veterinarian can recommend a vaccination schedule appropriate for your dog, taking into consideration the factors of climate and geography. The basic vaccinations to protect your dog are: parvovirus, distemper, hepatitis, leptospirosis, adenovirus, parainfluenza, coronavirus, bordetella, tracheobronchitis (kennel cough), Lyme disease and rabies.

Parvovirus is a highly contagious, dog-specific disease, first recognized in 1978. Targeting the small intestine, parvo affects the stomach, and diarrhea and vomiting (with blood) are clinical signs. Although the dog can pass the infection to other dogs within three days of infection, the initial signs, which include lethargy and depression, don't display themselves until four to seven days. When affecting puppies under four weeks of age, the heart muscle is frequently attacked. When the heart is affected, the puppies exhibit difficulty in breathing and experience crying and foaming at the nose and mouth.

Distemper, related to human measles, is an airborne virus that spreads in the blood and ultimately in the nervous system and epithelial tissues. Young dogs or dogs with weak immune systems can develop encephalomyelitis (brain disease) from the distemper infection. Such dogs experience seizures, general weakness and rigidity, as well as "hardpad". Since distemper is largely incurable, prevention through vaccination is vitally important. Puppies should be vaccinated at six to eight weeks of age, with boosters at ten to 12 weeks. Older puppies (16 weeks and older) who are unvaccinated should receive no fewer than two vaccinations at three- to four-week intervals.

Hepatitis mainly affects the liver and is caused by canine adenovirus type I. Highly infectious, hepatitis often affects dogs nine to 12 months of age. Initially the virus localizes in the dog's tonsils and then disperses to the liver, kidney and eyes. Generally speaking the dog's immune system is capable of combating this virus. Canine infectious hepatitis affects dogs whose systems cannot fight off the adenovirus. Affected dogs have fever, abdominal pains, bruising on mucous membranes and gums, and experience coma and convulsions. Prevention of hepatitis exists only through vaccination at eight to ten weeks of age and then boosters three or four weeks later, then annually.

Leptospirosis is a bacterium-related disease, often spread by rodents. The organisms that spread leptospirosis enter through the mucous membranes and spread to the internal organs via the bloodstream. It can be passed through the dog's urine. Leptospirosis does not affect young dogs as consistently as the other viruses do; it is reportedly regional in distribution and somewhat dependent on the immunostatus of the dog. Fever, inappetence, vomiting, dehydration, hemorrhaging, kidney and eye disease can result in moderate cases.

Bordetella, commonly refered to as canine cough, causes a persistent hacking cough in dogs and is very contagious. Bordetella involves a virus and a bacteria: parainfluenza is the most common virus implicated; *Bordetella bronchiseptica,* the bacterium. Bronchitis and pneumonia result in less than 20 percent of the cases, and most dogs recover from the condition within a week to four weeks. Non-prescription medicines can help relieve the hacking cough, though nothing can cure the condition before it's run its course. Vaccination cannot guarantee protection from canine cough, but it does ward off the most common virus responsible for the condition.

Lyme disease (also called borreliosis), although known for decades, was only first diagnosed in dogs in 1984. Lyme disease can affect cats, cattle, and horses, but especially people. In the U.S., the disease is transmitted by two ticks carrying the *Borrelia burgdorferi* organism: the deer tick (*Ixodes scapularis*) and the western black-legged tick (*Ixodes pacificus*), the latter primarily affects reptiles. In Europe, *Ixodes ricinus* is responsible for spreading Lyme. The disease causes lameness, fever, joint swelling, inappetence, and lethargy. Removal of ticks from the dog's coat can help reduce the chances of Lyme, though not as much as avoiding heavily wooded areas where the dog is most likely to contract ticks. A vaccination is available, though it has not been proven to protect dogs from all strains of the organism that cause the disease.

Rabies is passed to dogs and people through wildlife: in North America, principally through the skunk, fox and raccoon; the bat is not the culprit it was once thought to be. Likewise, the common image of the rabid dog foaming at the mouth with every hair on end is unlikely the truest scenario. A rabid dog exhibits difficulty eating, salivates much and has spells of paralysis and awkwardness. Before a dog reaches this final state, it may experience anxiety, personality changes, irritability and more aggressiveness than is usual. Vaccinations are strongly recommended as rabid dogs are too dangerous to manage and are commonly euthanized. Puppies are generally vaccinated at 12 weeks of age, and then annually. Although rabies is on the decline in the world community, tens of thousands of humans die each year from rabies-related incidents.

Parasites have clung to our pets for centuries. Despite our modern efforts, fleas still pester our pet's existence, and our own. All dogs itch, and fleas can make even the happiest dog a miserable, scabby mess. The loss of hair and habitual biting and chewing at themselves rank among the annoyances; the nuisances include the passing of tapeworms and the whole family's itching through the summer months. A full range of flea-control and elimination products are available at pet shops, and your veterinarian surely has recommendations. Sprays, powders, collars and dips fight fleas from the outside; drops and pills fight the good fight from inside. Discuss the possibilities with your vet. Not all products can be used in conjunction with one another, and some dogs may be more sensitive to certain applications than others. The dog's living quarters must be debugged as well as the dog itself. Heavy infestation may require multiple treatment.

Always check your dog for ticks carefully. Although fleas can be acquired almost anywhere, ticks are more likely to be picked up in heavily treed areas, pastures or other outside grounds (such as dog shows or obedience or field trials). Athletic, active, and hunting dogs are the most likely subjects, though any passing dog can be the host. Remember Lyme disease is passed by tick infestation.

As for internal parasites, worms are potentially dangerous for dogs and people. Roundworms, hookworms, whipworms, tapeworms, and heartworms comprise the blightsome party of troublemakers. Deworming puppies begins at around two to three weeks and continues until three months of age. Proper hygienic care of the environment is also important to prevent contamination with roundworm and hookworm eggs. Heartworm preventatives are recommended by most veterinarians, although there are some drawbacks to the regular introduction of poisons into our dogs' system. These daily or monthly preparations also help regulate most other worms as well. Discuss worming procedures with your veterinarian.

Roundworms pose a great threat to dogs and people. They are found in the intestine of dogs, and can be passed to people through ingestion of feces-contaminated dirt. Roundworm infection can be prevented by not walking dogs in heavy-traffic people areas, by burning feces, and by curbing dogs in a responsible manner. (Of course, in most areas of the country, curbing dogs is the law.) Roundworms are typically passed from the bitch to the litter, and bitches should be treated along with the puppies, even if she tested negative prior to whelping. Generally puppies are treated every two weeks until two months of age.

Hookworms, like roundworms, are also a danger to dogs and people. The hookworm parasite (known as *Ancylostoma caninum*) causes cutaneous larva migrans in people. The eggs of hookworms are passed in feces and become infective in shady, sandy areas.

The larvae penetrate the skin of the dog, and the dog subsequently becomes infected. When swallowed, these parasites affect the intestines, lungs, windpipe, and the whole digestive system. Infected dogs suffer from anemia and lose large amounts of blood in the places where the worms latch onto the dog's intestines, etc.

Although infrequently passed to humans, whipworms are cited as one of the most common parasites in America. These elongated worms affect the intestines of the dog, where they latch on, and cause colic upset or diarrhea. Unless identified in stools passed, whipworms are difficult to diagnose. Adult worms can be eliminated more consistently than the larvae, since whipworms exhibit unusual life cycles. Proper hygienic care of outdoor grounds is critical to the avoidance of these harmful parasites.

Tapeworms are carried by fleas, and enter the dog when the dog swallows the flea. Humans can acquire tapeworms in the same way, though we are less likely to swallow fleas than dogs are. Recent studies have shown that certain rodents and wild animals have been infected with tapeworms, and dogs can be affected by catching and/or eating these other animals. Of course, outdoor hunting dogs and terriers are more likely to be infected in this way than are your typical house dog or non-motivated hound. Treatment for tapeworms has proven very effective, and infected dogs do not show great discomfort or symptoms. When people are infected, however, the liver can be seriously damaged. Proper cleanliness is the best bet against tapeworms.

Heartworm disease is transmitted by mosquitoes and badly affects the lungs, heart and blood vessels of dogs. The larvae of *Dirofilaria immitis* enters the dog's bloodstream when bitten by an infected mosquito. The larvae takes about six months to mature. Infected dogs suffer from weight loss, appetite loss, chronic coughing and general fatigue. Not all affected dogs show signs of illness right away, and carrier dogs may be affected for years before clinical signs appear. Treatment of heartworm disease has been effective but can be dangerous also. Prevention as always is the desirable alternative. Ivermectin is the active ingredient in most heartworm preventatives and has proven to be successful. Check with your veterinarian for the preparation best for your dog. Dogs generally begin taking the preventatives at eight months of age and continue to do so throughout the non-winter months.

Tapeworms are carried by fleas which the dog swallows when biting himself.

FEEDING

Now let's talk about feeding your Doberman Pinscher, a subject so simple that it's amazing there is so much nonsense and misunderstanding about it. Is it expensive to feed a Doberman Pinscher? No, it is not! You can feed your Doberman Pinscher economically and keep him in perfect shape the year round, or you can feed him expensively. He'll thrive either way, and let's see why this is true.

First of all, remember a Doberman Pinscher is a dog. Dogs do not have a high degree of selectivity in their food, and unless you spoil them with great variety (and possibly turn them into poor, "picky" eaters) they will eat almost anything that they become accustomed to. Many dogs flatly refuse to eat nice, fresh beef. They pick around it and eat everything else. But meat—bah! Why? They aren't accustomed to it! They'd eat rabbit fast enough, but they refuse beef because they aren't used to it.

VARIETY NOT NECESSARY

A good general rule of thumb is forget all human preferences and don't give a thought to variety. Choose the right diet for your Doberman Pinscher and feed it to him day after day, year after year, winter and summer. But what is the right diet?

Hundreds of thousands of dollars have been spent in canine nutrition research. The results are pretty conclusive, so you needn't go into a lot of experimenting with trials of this and that every other week. Research has proven just what your dog needs to eat and to keep healthy.

DOG FOOD

There are almost as many right diets as there are dog experts, but the basic diet most often recommended is one that consists of a dry food, either meal or kibble form. There are several of these of excellent quality, manufactured by reliable companies, research tested, and nationally advertised. They are inexpensive, highly satisfactory, and easily available in stores everywhere in containers of five to 50 pounds. Larger amounts cost less per pound, usually.

If you have a choice of brands, it is usually safer to choose the better known one; but even so, carefully read the analysis on the package. Do not choose any food in which the protein level is less than 25 percent, and be sure that this protein comes from both animal and vegetable sources. The good dog foods have meat meal, fish meal, liver, and such, plus protein from alfalfa and soybeans, as well as some dried-milk product. Note the vitamin content carefully. See that they are all there in good proportions; and be especially certain that the food contains properly high levels of vitamins A and D, two of the most perishable and important ones. Note the B-complex level, but don't worry about carbohydrate and mineral levels. These substances are plentiful and cheap and not likely to be lacking in a good brand.

The advice given for how to choose a dry food also applies to moist or canned types of dog foods, if you decide to feed one of these.

Having chosen a really good food, feed it to your Doberman Pinscher as the manufacturer directs. And once you've started, stick to it. Never change if you can possibly help it. A switch from one meal or kibble-type food can usually be made without too much upset; however, a change will almost invariably give you (and your Doberman Pinscher) some trouble.

WHEN SUPPLEMENTS ARE NEEDED

Now what about supplements of various kinds, mineral and vitamin, or the various oils?

ISABELLE FRANCAIS

Because a Doberman puppy picks up a feather, it doesn't mean he's hungry. You should NOT allow your puppy to pick up strange things. They might be poisonous or carry disease.

They are all okay to add to your Doberman Pinscher's food. However, if you are feeding your Doberman Pinscher a correct diet, and this is easy to do, no supplements are necessary unless your Doberman Pinscher has been improperly fed, has been sick, or is having puppies. Vitamins and minerals are naturally present in all the foods; and to ensure against any loss through processing, they are added in concentrated form to the dog food you use. Except on the advice of your veterinarian, extra and added amounts of vitamins can prove harmful to your Doberman Pinscher! The same risk goes with minerals.

FEEDING SCHEDULE

When and how much food to give your Doberman Pinscher? As to when (except in the instance of puppies), suit yourself. You may feed two meals per day or the same amount in one single feeding, either morning or night. As to how to prepare the food and how much to give, it is generally best to follow the directions on the food package. Your own Doberman Pinscher may want a little more or a little less.

Fresh, cool water should always be available to your Doberman Pinscher. This is important to good health throughout his lifetime.

ALL DOBERMAN PINSCHERS NEED TO CHEW

Puppies and young Doberman Pinschers need something with resistance to chew on while their teeth and jaws are developing— for cutting the puppy teeth, to induce growth of the permanent teeth under the puppy teeth, to assist in getting rid of the puppy teeth at the proper time, to help the permanent teeth through the gums, to ensure normal jaw development, and to settle the permanent teeth solidly in the jaws.

The adult Doberman Pinscher's desire to chew stems from the instinct for tooth cleaning, gum massage, and jaw exercise—plus the need for an outlet for periodic doggie tensions.

This is why dogs, especially puppies and young dogs, will often destroy property worth hundreds of dollars when their chewing instinct is not diverted from their owner's possessions. And this is why you should provide your Doberman Pinscher with something to chew— something that has the necessary functional qualities, is desirable from the Doberman Pinscher's viewpoint, and is safe for him.

It is very important that your Doberman Pinscher not be permitted to chew on anything he can break or on any indigestible thing from which he can bite sizable chunks. Sharp pieces, such as from a bone which can be broken by a dog, may pierce the intestinal wall and kill. Indigestible things that can be bitten off in chunks, such as from shoes or rubber or plastic toys, may cause an intestinal stoppage (if not regurgitated) and bring painful death, unless surgery is promptly performed.

Strong natural bones, such as 4- to 8-inch lengths of round shin bone from mature beef— either the kind you can get from a butcher or one of the variety available commercially in pet stores—may serve your Doberman Pinscher's teething needs if his mouth is large enough to handle them effectively. You may be tempted to give your Doberman Pinscher puppy a smaller bone and he may not be able to break it when you do, but puppies grow rapidly and the power of their jaws constantly increases until maturity. This means that a growing Doberman Pinscher may break one of the smaller bones at any time, swallow the pieces, and die painfully before you realize what is wrong.

All hard natural bones are very abrasive. If your Doberman Pinscher is an avid chewer, natural bones may wear away his teeth prematurely; hence, they should be taken away from your dog when the teething purposes have been served. The

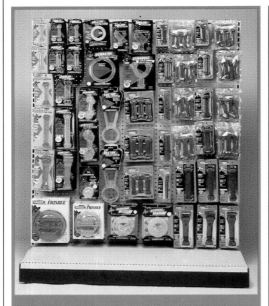

Most pet shops have complete walls dedicated to safe pacifiers.

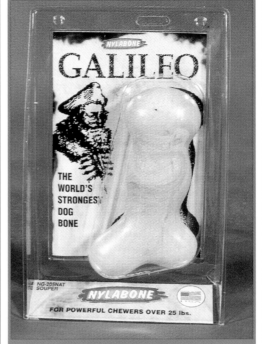

The Galileo is an extremely tough nylon pacifier. Its design is based upon original sketches by Galileo. A book explaining the history and workings of the design come inside each package. This might very well be the best design for Dobermans.

Dobermans have such strong jaws that most ordinary pacifiers (chew devices) are immediately destroyed. The Hercules has been designed with Dobermans and other large breeds in mind. This bone is made of polyurethane, like car bumpers.

Raised dental tips on each dog bone works wonders with controlling plaque in Dobermans.

Only get the largest plaque attacker for your Doberman.

badly worn, and usually painful, teeth of many mature dogs can be traced to excessive chewing on natural bones.

Contrary to popular belief, knuckle bones that can be chewed up and swallowed by your Doberman Pinscher provide little, if any, usable calcium or other nutrients. They do, however, disturb the digestion of most dogs and cause them to vomit the nourishing food they need.

Dried rawhide products of various types, shapes, sizes, and prices are available on the market and have become quite popular.

However, they don't serve the primary chewing functions very well; they are a bit messy when wet from mouthing, and most Doberman Pinschers chew them up rather rapidly— but they have been considered safe for dogs until recently. Now, more and more incidents of death, and near death, by strangulation have been reported to be the results of partially swallowed chunks of rawhide swelling in the throat. More recently, some veterinarians have been attributing cases of acute constipation to large pieces of incompletely digested rawhide in the intestine.

A new product, molded rawhide, is very safe. During the process, the rawhide is melted and then injection molded into the familiar dog shape. It is very hard and is eagerly accepted by Doberman Pinschers. The melting process also sterilizes the rawhide. Don't confuse this with pressed rawhide, which is nothing more than small strips of rawhide squeezed together.

The nylon bones, especially those with natural meat and bone fractions added, are probably the most complete, safe, and economical answer to the chewing need. Dogs cannot break them or bite off sizable chunks; hence, they are completely safe—and being longer lasting than other things offered for the purpose, they are economical.

Hard chewing raises little bristle-like projections on the surface of the nylon bones—to

hambone scented

GUMABONE

POOCH PACIFIER

SAVES MONEY & DOGS' LIVES

PLAY TOY & EXERCISER

LASTS 10 TIMES LONGER THAN RAWHIDE

GIANT-SIZE
For Large Dogs

"WHY"
On Reverse Side
!

The Nylabone/Gumabone Pooch Pacifiers enable the dog to slowly chew off the knobs while they clean their own teeth. The knobs develop elastic frays which act as a toothbrush. These pacifiers are extremely effective as detailed scientific studies have shown.

provide effective interim tooth cleaning and vigorous gum massage, much in the same way your toothbrush does it for you. The little projections are raked off and swallowed in the form of thin shavings, but the chemistry of the nylon is such that they break down in the stomach fluids and pass through without effect.

The toughness of the nylon provides the strong chewing resistance needed for important jaw exercise and effectively aids teething functions, but there is no tooth wear because nylon is non-abrasive. Being inert, nylon does not support the growth of microorganisms; and it can be washed in soap and water or it can be sterilized by boiling or in an autoclave.

Nylabone® is highly recommended by veterinarians as a safe, healthy nylon bone that can't splinter or chip. Nylabone® is frizzled by the dog's chewing action, creating a

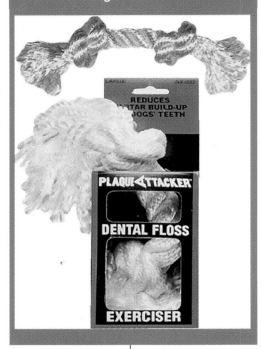

The nylon tug toy is actually a dental floss. You grab one end and let your Doberman tug on the other as it slowly slips through his teeth since nylon is self-lubricating (slippery). Do NOT use cotton rope tug toys as cotton is organic and rots. It is also weak and easily loses strands which are indigestible should the dog swallow them.

toothbrush-like surface that cleanses the teeth and massages the gums. Nylabone®, the only chew products made of flavor-impregnated solid nylon, are available in your local pet shop. Nylabone® is superior to the cheaper bones because it is made of virgin nylon, which is the strongest and longest-lasting type of nylon available. The cheaper bones are made from recycled or re-ground nylon scraps, and have a tendency to break apart and split easily.

Nothing, however, substitutes for periodic professional attention for your Doberman Pinscher's teeth and gums, not any more than your toothbrush can do that for you. Have your Doberman Pinscher's teeth cleaned at least once a year by your veterinarian (twice a year is better) and he will be happier, healthier, and far more pleasant to live with.